RAND

The Role of the Office of Homeland Security in the Federal Budget Process

Recommendations for Effective Long-Term Engagement

Victoria A. Greenfield

Prepared for
The RAND Corporation

National Security Research Division

This research was conducted by RAND as part of its continuing program of self-sponsored research. RAND acknowledges the support for such research provided by the independent research and development (IR&D) provisions of RAND's contracts for the operation of its Department of Defense federally funded research and development centers.

Library of Congress Cataloging-in-Publication Data

Greenfield, Victoria A., 1964–
    The role of the Office of Homeland Security in the federal budget process :
recommendations for effective long-term engagement / Victoria A. Greenfield.
        p. cm.
    Includes bibliographical references.
    "MR-1573."
    ISBN 0-8330-3188-0
    1. United States. Office of Homeland Security—Finance. 2. Budget—United States.
I.Title.

HV6432 .G74 2002
353.9'5—dc21

                                                                    2002069771

RAND is a nonprofit institution that helps improve policy and decisionmaking through research and analysis. RAND® is a registered trademark. RAND's publications do not necessarily reflect the opinions or policies of its research sponsors.

Published 2002 by RAND
1700 Main Street, P.O. Box 2138, Santa Monica, CA 90407-2138
1200 South Hayes Street, Arlington, VA 22202-5050
201 North Craig Street, Suite 102, Pittsburgh, PA 15213-1516
RAND URL: http://www.rand.org/
To order RAND documents or to obtain additional information, contact Distribution
Services: Telephone: (310) 451-7002; Fax: (310) 451-6915; Email: order@rand.org

Preface

This RAND-sponsored study is intended to inform the discussion of the Office of Homeland Security's (OHS's) engagement in the federal budget process. Our recommendations for interagency strategy and funding coordination are based on an analysis of expert opinion, institutional analogy, and congressional interest and involvement, as reflected in funding streams, committee hearings, and referrals of legislative proposals. The research for this study was initiated in December 2001 and completed in February 2002.

Our analysis suggests that OHS can engage effectively in the budget process in its current institutional form, but it must build on the strength of its relationship with the President over the longer term. Defining efficacy as the ability of OHS to secure department and agency funding for agreed programs and activities in support of the President's policy agenda, we identify key points of leverage inside and outside government and also recommend specific mechanisms for participating in the executive branch and congressional phases of the budget process. It is our view that OHS will be most effective if it treats interagency strategy and funding coordination in tandem, through an integrated framework that focuses on core cross-cutting policy issues and that is tied to the budget cycle. We develop a framework that starts with policy priorities and objectives and then flows to strategy formulation and funding requests, clearly mapping budget proposals to specific programs and activities. This report should be of interest to those involved in the debate on the coordination of homeland security strategy and funding, including policymakers in the executive branch, members of Congress, and their staff.

Our data on committee hearings, legislative proposals, and funding streams are descriptive, but not definitive. We exercised considerable judgment in determining which committee hearings and legislative proposals were related to homeland security, finding record of over 200 such hearings between January 1999 and December 2001 and about 180 such proposals in 2001 alone. To weigh the interest and involvement of the appropriators, we apportioned the departments' and agencies' FY 2001, FY 2002, and proposed FY 2003 homeland security funding to their corresponding appropriations subcommittees.

This study was conducted by RAND as part of its continuing program of self-sponsored research. We acknowledge the support for such research provided by the independent research and development provisions of RAND's contracts for the operation of its Department of Defense federally funded research and development centers: Project AIR FORCE (sponsored by the U.S. Air Force), the Arroyo Center (sponsored by the U.S. Army), and the National Defense Research Institute (sponsored by the Office of the Secretary of Defense, the Joint Staff, the unified commands, and the defense agencies).

This research was overseen by RAND's National Security Research Division (NSRD). NSRD conducts research and analysis for the Office of the Secretary of Defense, the Joint Staff, the unified commands, the defense agencies, the Department of the Navy, the U.S. intelligence community, allied foreign governments, and foundations.

Contents

Figures

Tables

Summary

Executive Order 13228 established the Office of Homeland Security (OHS) as an advisory body in the Executive Office of the President (EOP) to "coordinate the executive branch's efforts to detect, prepare for, prevent, respond to, and recover from, terrorist attacks within the United States." The executive order also tasks OHS with a Budget Review, stating that the Assistant to the President for Homeland Security—also called the Homeland Security Director or OHS Director—shall consult with and provide advice to the department and agency heads and the Office of Management and Budget (OMB) Director on homeland security programs, activities, and funding. The executive order does not provide specific mechanisms for participation in the federal budget process, other than the OHS Director's certification of "necessary and appropriate" funding levels.

Taking the institutional standing of OHS as given, we propose specific mechanisms for its effective long-term engagement in the executive branch and congressional phases of the budget process. We define efficacy as the ability of OHS to secure department and agency funding for agreed programs and activities in support of the President's homeland security agenda. It is our view that OHS will be most successful if it treats strategy and funding coordination in tandem, through an integrated framework or interagency policy process keyed to the budget cycle. While recognizing that OHS must be comprehensive in its coverage, we recommend that it focus on core issues along the "seams" of homeland security policy. Issues at the nexus of two or more departments' or agencies' jurisdictions, such as border security or bioterrorism, will provide the greatest challenges and payoffs because they require coordination rather than monitoring.

Our recommendations are based on an analysis of expert opinion, institutional analogy, and congressional activity. We conducted a series of informal interviews with budget, policy, and legal experts, including former and current administration officials and congressional staff; reviewed the experience of other EOP offices with interagency leadership roles, such as the National Security Council (NSC), National Economic Council (NEC), and Office of National Drug Control Policy (ONDCP); and assessed congressional interest and involvement in homeland security issues, as reflected in funding streams, referrals of legislative proposals, and degree of initiative by specific congressional committees and subcommittees.

The results of our analysis suggest that OHS can engage effectively in its current form, but will need to build on the foundation of its presidential imprimatur, particularly as the nation's sense of urgency from the events of September 11, 2001, fades. In this report, we discuss opportunities for OHS to leverage strong working relationships with other key players in the administration, Congress, and outside the federal government; we also develop a model for interagency strategy and funding coordination that builds on those relationships. Although our approach is issue based, it is not issue specific. We present a generic template for coordination that can be adapted to almost any cross-cutting policy issue, using the structure of the Homeland Security Council (HSC) provided in Homeland Security Presidential Directive–1 (HSPD-1). From top to bottom, that structure consists of a cabinet-level Principals Committee (HSC/PC), chaired by the OHS Director; a subcabinet-level Deputies Committee (HSC/DC); and several Policy Coordination Committees (HSC/PCCs) organized by topic, with subordinate working groups.

Building Relationships

With the President's full support as a prerequisite, OHS can leverage its position in the EOP by cultivating and managing its relationships with other homeland security institutions and their proponents. They are

- Other executive branch entities, particularly OMB and the NSC
- Congress, including, but not limited to, the appropriators
- State, local, and nongovernmental leadership
- The American press and public.

We focus on relationships within the federal government, addressing how they change over the course of the budget cycle, and consider others with nonfederal entities, including state, local, and nongovernmental leadership. Not surprisingly, the relationship between OHS and OMB is especially important. OMB coordinates the executive branch budget process and can also provide OHS with technical assistance. However, this relationship may reach "natural" limits owing to differences in the offices' missions, which become most apparent when resources are scarce. Strong working relationships with the NSC and other departments and agencies, per Executive Order 13228 and HSPD-1, are also important.

After the President submits his plan to Congress, the fate of homeland security funding rests largely, but not entirely, with the appropriators. First, the debate goes to the Budget Committees, offering OHS a rare opportunity to present a unified policy perspective. Later, the debate becomes more fragmented when the appropriators consider funding along their jurisdictional lines. Although nearly all 13 subcommittees have some financial control over homeland security policy, our analysis of FY 2001, FY 2002, and proposed FY 2003 funding indicates that six tend to account for most of the appropriations (Figure S1). Four subcommittees—Defense; Commerce, Justice, State, and the Judiciary; Transportation; and Treasury, Postal, and General Government—were prominent in all three years. Two others—Labor, Health and Human Services, and Education; and Veterans Affairs, Housing and Urban Development, and Independent Agencies—emerged later. OHS can work with the appropriators, both directly and indirectly, through the President, OMB, and departments and agencies to promote agreed administration positions.

However, even before the congressional budget process begins, OHS can reach out to interested members and their staffs through briefings and other informal channels. OHS can proceed strategically: first, forming alliances with "core"

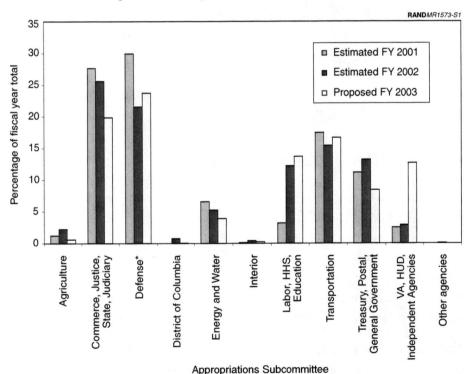

NOTE: Derived from OMB Department and Agency Estimates and Requests as of February 2002, with FY 2001 and FY 2002 Supplemental Funding.
*Funding attributed to the Defense Subcommittee may include some funding ordinarily associated with the Military Construction Subcommittee.

Figure S1—Approximate Shares of Discretionary Homeland Security Funding by Appropriations Subcommittee

committees that have been most interested and involved in homeland security policy, and, later, casting a wider net to expand its network. Our analysis of the frequency of committees' pre– and post–September 11 hearings and referrals of recent legislative proposals suggests a starting point. A modest number of committees have been active generally; others have also entered the field since the attacks or have focused more narrowly on specific issues within their jurisdictions.

Which committees form the core? Apart from the appropriators, our analysis of both hearings and referrals points to two Senate committees—the Judiciary and Commerce, Science, and Transportation—and three House committees— Transportation and Infrastructure, the Judiciary, and Energy and Commerce. Looking only at their hearings and not referrals, we find that the House Government Reform Committee is also a clear leader; more recently, the Senate Governmental Affairs Committee has also stepped in. Some other committees have joined debates on specific issues, but would not make the top ranks otherwise. For example, the Senate Health, Education, Labor, and Pensions Committee and the House Agriculture Committee have seen more bioterrorism-related proposals than most committees. The Senate and House Armed Services Committees, although less visible than others since September 11 by these measures, warrant attention both because their past activity indicates long-term interest and because they are among the few authorizing committees to exercise influence within their domains, on par with the corresponding appropriators.

Coordinating Strategy and Funding

Ultimately, the budgetary effectiveness of OHS will depend on how it uses its EOP position and what it brings to the interagency table. OHS must understand the workings of the budget process and fill a role that the departments and agencies cannot satisfy independently, such as policy coordination, where their authorities overlap or gap. Speaking on behalf of the President, OHS is uniquely poised to bring strategy and funding decisions together across departments and agencies and provide a unified White House perspective on homeland security.

Our analysis yields three key, if deceptively simple, principles for effective budgetary engagement, which we fold into a proposed road map for interagency strategy and funding coordination using the HSC structure:

- Establish policy priorities and objectives as early as possible

- Formulate strategy and then develop funding requests

- Be prepared for rapid change.

Here and in Table S1, we introduce a framework that weds an ONDCP-like timetable to an NSC/NEC–like approach to policy coordination. Ideally, a tightly run interagency process would flow from policy priorities and objectives, to strategy formulation, to funding requests—clearly mapping requests to specific programs and activities. OHS must articulate the President's policy agenda as early as possible, setting priorities and objectives for the coming year in the context of a longer-term strategy. In the spring before the next budget submission (e.g., in 2002 for the FY 2004 budget), OHS should engage OMB, the NSC, and the key departments and agencies through the HSC/PC to gain institutional buy-in or, at least, awareness. With this cabinet-level support, OHS would lead HSC/PCCs and working groups to formulate strategy and to identify gaps and redundancies in programs, activities, and funding. Proposals and options would percolate up through the HSC structure for decision. From the start, direct access to departments' and agencies' internal planning and decisionmaking processes would be advantageous. Moreover, coordination with nonfederal entities would be necessary to assure the strategy's consistency and operability at different levels.

OHS would use this top-to-bottom-to-top approach to reach closure with the departments and agencies before their formal OMB budget requests and certification. However, OHS should continue to engage through and beyond the final phases of the executive branch process. This requires direct access to senior-level reviews, including passback and appeals, and the President. Finally, the homeland security threat is dynamic. If conditions change abruptly, OHS must be able to shift gears quickly and bring departments and agencies along with it. A well-functioning interagency strategy and funding coordination process would facilitate the response.

Our emphasis is on issue-based interagency coordination. We believe that OHS can be effective in this role in its current institutional form. However, OHS will likely have an easier time as a coordinator to the extent that it still benefits from political goodwill, in both the executive branch and Congress, and while funding is readily available—departments and agencies tend to be more cooperative when real resources are on the table. If OHS can establish a policy process when goodwill and resources are on its side, it may be able to carry over that process into leaner times.

Table S1

Proposed OHS Activity in the Executive Budget Process

	Calendar Year Prior to the Year in Which Fiscal Year Begins		
Time Period	*Current Executive Branch Activity* General[a]	ONDCP[b]	Proposed OHS Activity
Feb.–March	N/A	ONDCP issues National Drug Control Strategy, including strategic goals and objectives.	OHS specifies objectives and priorities, focusing on core issues that require interagency coordination; convenes cabinet-level interagency meeting through HSC/PC, with OMB and NSC directors attending, to set policy agenda.
April–June	Agencies begin development of budget requests. The President, with the assistance of OMB, reviews and makes policy decisions for the budget that begins October 1 of the following year.	ONDCP issues process guidance to departmental budget directors, augmenting the general policy guidance provided in the National Strategy; meets with senior budget officials from departments and agencies; develops and proposes agency drug initiatives; issues additional guidance to cabinet officers on funding priorities for specific initiatives; begins summer budget certification and review process for certain agencies, bureaus, and programs.	OHS leads issue-based HSC/PCCs and IWGs, with OMB and NSC participation, to formulate and coordinate interagency strategy and identify funding requirements for programs and activities; coordinates with FEMA and consults advisory committees and associations for state, local, and private sector input at HSC/PCC level; presents proposal or options to HSC/DC or HSC/PC.
July–Aug.	OMB issues policy directions to agencies, providing guidance for agencies' formal budget requests.	ONDCP continues summer budget process; prepares pre-certification letters for departments; meets with cabinet officers to discuss funding priorities prior to OMB submission.	Agencies prepare preliminary budget proposals, linking funding to strategy through agreed programs and activities; OHS policy and budget staff review preliminary proposals with OMB staff assistance; OHS presents unified perspective to HSC/PCCs and IWGs, using meetings to

Table S1—continued

Time Period	General[a]	ONDCP[b]	Proposed OHS Activity
July–Aug. (cont.)			address conflicts, gaps, etc., and raises any unresolved issues to the HSC/DC or HSC/PC if needed; checks for consistency with OMB aggregate funding report.
Early fall	Agencies submit initial budget requests to OMB.	ONDCP begins fall budget certification review process; receiving departments' proposals prior to OMB.	OHS staff reviews agencies' formal budget submissions, working closely with OMB staff, and certifies adequacy to OMB Director.
Nov.–Dec.	OMB and the President review and make decisions on agencies' requests, referred to as OMB "passback"; following passback, agencies identify shortfalls and prioritize appeals; agencies may appeal these decision to the OMB Director, and in some cases directly to the President.	ONDCP issues certification letters and makes final budget recommendations.	OHS participates in senior-level reviews with OMB and NSC; OHS works with agencies after passback, one-on-one or together, to identify remaining shortfalls and prioritize appeals; OHS petitions the President directly if necessary.

Calendar Year in Which Fiscal Year Begins			
Time Period	*Current Executive Branch Activity*		Proposed OHS Activity
	General[a]	ONDCP[b]	
February	President submits budget—no later than the first Monday of February—to Congress; OMB coordinates roll out.	ONDCP issues National Drug Control Strategy, including proposed national drug control budget.	OHS provides executive support and engages in public outreach through speeches, press statements, fact sheets, etc., presenting unified policy perspective.

Table S1—continued

Time Period	General[a]	ONDCP[b]	Proposed OHS Activity
Feb.– Sept.	Congressional phase: Agencies interact with Congress, justifying and explaining President's budget.	Congressional phase: Agencies interact with Congress, justifying and explaining President's budget.	OHS briefs Congress, including but not limited to the leadership and appropriating committees, and interacts indirectly, through the President, OMB, and departments and agencies.
October 1	Fiscal year begins.	Fiscal year begins.	Fiscal year begins.
Oct.– Sept.	OMB apportions funds to agencies. Agencies incur obligations and make outlays.	—	OHS monitors strategy; develops supplemental requests with OMB and through the interagency coordination process, as necessary.

[a]From Heniff (1999).

[b]From U.S. General Accounting Office (1999).

NOTE: FEMA = Federal Emergency Management Agency; HSC = Homeland Security Council; HSC/PC = HSC/Principals Committee; HSC/DC = HSC/Deputies Committee; HSC/PCC = HSC/Policy Coordination Committee; IWG = interagency working group; OHS = Office of Homeland Security; OMB = Office of Management and Budget; ONDCP = Office of National Drug Control Policy. HSC/PCCs are organized topically. The chairman of each HSC/PCC may establish subordinate IWGs to assist the HSC/PCC.

Acknowledgments

We gratefully acknowledge Lowell Schwartz for his assistance in researching and producing the database on congressional hearings and Jessica Kmiec and David Howell for their assistance developing the database on legislative proposals. Shirley Ruhe helped us obtain essential budget data. Mary DeRosa provided input on some important legal issues. Frances Lussier and Patrick Murphy, who reviewed the draft, provided technical and presentational suggestions that greatly improved the final product. We also thank the many policy, budget, and legal experts, including former and current administration officials and congressional staff, who contributed their valuable time to informal interviews when they had very little time to spare.

We take full responsibility for any errors or omissions.

Abbreviations

EOP	Executive Office of the President
FEMA	Federal Emergency Management Agency
FOIA	Freedom of Information Act
FY	Fiscal year
HHS	U.S. Department of Health and Human Services
HSC	Homeland Security Council
HSC/DC	HSC/Deputies Committee
HSC/PC	HSC/Principals Committee
HSC/PCC	HSC/Policy Coordination Committee
HSPD-1	Homeland Security Presidential Directive–1
HUD	U.S. Department of Housing and Urban Development
IWG	Interagency working group
NEC	National Economic Council
NSC	National Security Council
OHS	Office of Homeland Security
OMB	Office of Management and Budget
ONDCP	Office of National Drug Control Policy
U.S.C.	United States Code
VA	U.S. Department of Veterans Affairs

1. Introduction

On October 8, 2001, President Bush created the Office of Homeland Security (OHS) by Executive Order 13228 to "coordinate the executive branch's efforts to detect, prepare for, prevent, respond to, and recover from, terrorist attacks within the United States." The executive order tasks OHS with wide-ranging functions and responsibilities, including a Budget Review:

> The Assistant to the President for Homeland Security, in consultation with the Director of the Office of Management and Budget (the "Director") and the heads of executive departments and agencies, shall identify programs that contribute to the Administration's strategy for homeland security and, in the development of the President's annual budget submission, shall review and provide advice to the heads of departments and agencies for such programs. The Assistant to the President for Homeland Security shall provide advice to the Director on the level and use of funding in departments and agencies for homeland security–related activities and, prior to the Director's forwarding of the proposed annual budget submission to the President for transmittal to the Congress, shall certify to the Director the funding levels that the Assistant to the President for Homeland Security believes are necessary and appropriate for the homeland security–related activities of the executive branch.

The executive order offers guidance on the role of OHS in the budget process, but does not provide a specific implementing mechanism other than a broadly worded call for certification: The Assistant to the President for Homeland Security—also called the Homeland Security Director or OHS Director—will certify the funding levels for homeland security that he believes are necessary and appropriate. The language of the executive order may be purposefully nonprescriptive to allow for administrative flexibility.

Selecting from many possible institutional arrangements, the President chose to place OHS within the Executive Office of the President (EOP), with influence deriving largely from proximity to the Oval Office, but not from independent authority—statutory or otherwise.[1] The OHS Director reports directly to the President. As an immediate adviser to the President, he does not require Senate confirmation nor can he be required to testify before Congress. And, acting as an

---

[1] Independent authority can derive from statute or presidential delegation.

adviser, without "substantial" independent authority, OHS is not subject to the Freedom of Information Act (FOIA), which sets forth extensive procedural requirements.[2]

OHS may be walking a fine line between institutional empowerment and autonomy. If OHS were endowed with substantial independent authority, regardless of the authority's source, it could be subject to FOIA; were the authority derived from statute, the Director could be required to testify. Moreover, the legal lines are not clearly drawn. Were OHS to appear to direct other departments' or agencies' programs, activities, or funding, or take on operational responsibilities, it could lose some of its autonomy, regardless of its EOP standing. However, the press continues to raise concerns as to whether OHS can effectively serve as a policy and budget coordinator absent a formal congressional mandate or more direct control over departments' and agencies' funding.[3]

This report responds to some of those concerns. Taking the institutional standing of OHS as an advisory body in the EOP as given, we provide the office with recommendations for its effective budgetary engagement in the periods both before and after the President submits his plan to Congress—i.e., the executive branch and congressional phases of the federal budget process. We define efficacy as the ability of OHS to secure department and agency funding for agreed programs and activities in support of the President's policy agenda.

To carry out our analysis, we conducted a series of informal interviews with budget, policy, and legal experts, including former and current administration officials and congressional staff; reviewed the experience of other EOP offices leading a wide range of interagency policy processes; and assessed congressional interest and involvement in homeland security, as reflected in funding streams, legislative proposals, and degree of initiative by specific congressional committees and subcommittees.

In reviewing the experience of other EOP offices, we sought reasonable institutional and functional analogies and looked most closely at the successes and failures of the NSC, National Economic Council (NEC), and Office of National Drug Control Policy (ONDCP).[4] Although none of these EOP offices is a perfect match, each fills a coordinating role that merits examination, and

---

[2]A federal appeals court has held that the National Security Council (NSC) has no "substantial" independent authority and, therefore, is not subject to FOIA.

[3]For example, see Pianin and Miller (2002) and Bettelheim (2002).

[4]For another possible analogy, see Relyea (2001) on the Office of War Mobilization and the Office of War Mobilization and Reconversion.

collectively they cover most of the relevant institutional and functional waterfront, at least among federal entities.

- The National Security Act of 1947 first established the NSC. Although created legislatively, the NSC does not have substantial independent authority.

  > The National Security Council is the President's principal forum for considering national security and foreign policy matters with his senior national security advisors and cabinet officials. Since its inception under President Truman, the function of the Council has been to advise and assist the President on national security and foreign policies. The Council also serves as the President's principal arm for coordinating these policies among various government agencies.[5]

  The Assistant to the President for National Security Affairs is not subject to Senate confirmation and, as an immediate adviser to the President, cannot be compelled to testify before Congress. Additionally, as an office within the EOP that has no substantial independent authority, the NSC is not subject to FOIA.

- The NEC arose administratively and, like the NSC, has no substantial independent authority.

  > The NEC was established in 1993 within the Office of Policy Development and is part of the [EOP]. It was created for the purpose of advising the President on matters related to U.S. and global economic policy. By Executive Order, the NEC has four principal functions: to coordinate policy-making for domestic and international economic issues, to coordinate economic policy advice for the President, to ensure that policy decisions and programs are consistent with the President's economic goals, and to monitor implementation of the President's economic policy agenda.[6]

- The Anti-Drug Abuse Act of 1988 established ONDCP. Per legislative mandate, ONDCP must

  > develop a national drug control policy; coordinate and oversee the implementation of that policy; assess and certify the adequacy of national drug control programs and the budget for those programs;

---

[5]See http://www.whitehouse.gov/nsc/ (information accessed February 6, 2002).

[6]See http://www.whitehouse.gov/nec/ (information accessed February 6, 2002). President Clinton established the NEC in 1993, but other previous administrations have established similar offices. For more on past incarnations, see Orszag, Orszag, and Tyson (2001).

and evaluate the effectiveness of the national drug control programs.[7]

Unlike the NSC or NEC, Congress has endowed ONDCP with substantial independent authority. Accordingly, the Senate confirms the ONDCP Director and Congress can call on the Director to testify. The office is also subject to FOIA.

Taken together, the positive and negative experiences of these EOP offices provide insight. Institutionally, OHS looks more like the NSC and NEC than ONDCP. Like OHS, both the NSC and NEC play their parts without substantial independent authority. They function as presidential advisory and policy coordinating bodies and derive no authority from statute. Indeed, although Congress had a hand in creating the NSC through the 1947 Act, the NEC arose entirely via presidential action. In contrast, Congress created ONDCP and the office has substantial independent authority derived from statute.

Functionally, OHS shares common ground with all three EOP offices, but there are yet differences among them. Clearly, each office coordinates policy across federal departments and agencies, although the NSC usually works with fewer departments and agencies than either the NEC or ONDCP. ONDCP also has much more contact with state, local, and private entities.[8] Regarding the budget process, the NSC and NEC tend to weigh in only to the extent that interagency policy coordination requires it—typically on a case-by-case basis. In comparison, ONDCP bears statutory responsibility for developing a consolidated budget to implement a National Drug Control Strategy, with formal mechanisms for engaging with departments and agencies in the federal budget process. ONDCP is also the administration's chief public spokesperson on drug control.[9] The NSC and NEC tend to be less visible, but no less authoritative.

The collective experience of the NSC, NEC, and ONDCP provides evidence that the key to success is not necessarily in the institutional standing of an office or its formal authority. The NSC and NEC have exercised considerable influence over policymaking writ large and within the budget process on a case-by-case basis, with no statutory authority; ONDCP has perhaps been less influential despite its

---

[7]See Section 703 of the Office of National Drug Control Policy Reauthorization Act of 1998. The act expanded the office's mandate and authority by specifying additional reporting requirements and responsibilities.

[8]For example, the Drug-Free Communities Act of 1997 authorized ONDCP to carry out a national initiative that awards federal grants directly to community coalitions in the United States.

[9]Building on this role, the Media Campaign Act of 1998 directed ONDCP to conduct a national media campaign to reduce and prevent drug abuse among young Americans.

legislative mandate.[10] Arguably, these offices' missions—and the challenges arising from them—are quite different; this does not mean, however, that we cannot draw any general conclusions from their experience. In fact, at least one basic insight emerges readily: The President's backing is essential—but other factors cannot be overlooked. The key to success is part process, part substance, and part human alchemy.

Taken as a whole, our analysis of expert opinion, institutional analogy, and congressional activity suggests that OHS can engage effectively in its current institutional form, but it must build on the foundation of its presidential imprimatur, especially over the longer term. It is our view that OHS will be most effective if it treats strategy and funding coordination in tandem, through an integrated framework or "interagency policy process" keyed to the federal budget cycle. While recognizing that OHS must be comprehensive in its coverage, we recommend that it focus its time and attention on core issues along the "seams" of homeland security policy.[11] Issues at the nexus of two or more departments' or agencies' jurisdictions, such as border security and bioterrorism, will provide the greatest challenges and payoffs because they require coordination, rather than monitoring. Among the challenges, addressing these issues may require a third party to mediate interagency conflict as it arises. This mediator could encourage departments and agencies to move beyond the status quo, especially when movement involves reallocating resources. OHS may be well positioned to do both.

In the sections that follow, we discuss opportunities for OHS to leverage strong working relationships with other key players in the administration, Congress, and elsewhere. We also develop a framework, or model, for effective long-term engagement that builds on those relationships. Our approach is issue based, but it is not issue specific. We provide a template for interagency strategy and funding coordination that can be adapted to any particular issue, using the structure of the Homeland Security Council (HSC) provided under the Homeland Security Presidential Directive–1 (HSPD-1). From the top down, the HSC structure consists of a cabinet-level Principals Committee (HSC/PC) chaired by the OHS Director, a subcabinet-level Deputies Committee (HSC/DC), and several Policy Coordination Committees (HSC/PCCs) organized along

---

[10]This observation derives from our assessment of interviewees' remarks and of written commentaries on the EOP offices under consideration, including Daalder and Destler (2001); Orszag, Orszag, and Tyson (2001); U.S. Department of State (1997); and U.S. General Accounting Office (1999).

[11]One interviewee offered a particularly clear articulation of this concept, including the term "seams," which we have incorporated in our discussion.

topical lines.[12] HSPD-1 also allows the chairman of each HSC/PCC to establish subordinate working groups (hereafter referred to as interagency working groups [IWGs]) to assist the HSC/PCC in the performance of its duties.[13]

In our discussion of strategy and funding coordination, we address the federal budget process in two distinct phases: (1) the executive branch phase, during which the departments and agencies develop their fiscal plans for the next budget under consideration, and (2) the congressional phase, during which Congress deliberates on the administration's proposal and eventually provides budget authority through appropriations acts. To a lesser extent, we also provide suggestions for coordinating with nonfederal entities. Not only are states, localities, and private entities on the front line of homeland security, but the funding that passes to them (through federal grants, loans, and other vehicles) generally derives from the same budget processes as the funding that federal departments and agencies spend directly.

---

[12]HSPD-1 identifies 11 HSC/PCCs: (1) detection, surveillance, and intelligence; (2) plans, training, exercises, and evaluation; (3) law enforcement and investigation; (4) weapons of mass destruction consequence management; (5) key asset, border, territorial waters, and airspace security; (6) domestic transportation security; (7) research and development; (8) medical and public health preparedness; (9) domestic threat response and incident management; (10) economic consequences; and (11) public affairs.

[13]Though not addressed in HSPD-1, an IWG could potentially accommodate issues that do not fall neatly within HSC/PCC lines. For a narrower discussion, an IWG could consist of a subset of participants' delegates from a particular HSC/PCC; for a broader discussion, it could include delegates from two or more HSC/PCCs, possibly requiring reports to multiple HSC/PCCs. Presumably, each IWG would require different participants from different departments and agencies, depending on its purpose (e.g., an IWG on bioterrorism would not have the same composition as an IWG on border control).

2. Key Relationships and Points of Leverage

One relationship ranks above all others in its importance. First and foremost, OHS requires the full support of the President. OHS cannot control an interagency process—or broker a budget deal—unless it is seen to be speaking on the President's behalf. However, OHS cannot rely solely on this relationship to engage effectively, day-to-day, over the longer term.[14] It must develop clout of its own, admittedly deriving partly from its relationships with other key players. When conflicts arise in the interagency process—and they inevitably will—OHS can invoke its presidential trump card, but only sparingly. Moreover, as a practicality, the President typically does not become involved in the budget process until the endgame and even then may delegate responsibility to the Chief of Staff or another EOP proxy, possibly the Office of Management and Budget (OMB) Director.[15] To effectively coordinate strategy and the funding to support it, OHS must become involved much earlier.

With the President's backing, OHS can leverage its EOP position, in part, by cultivating and managing its relationships with key institutions and their proponents. They are

- Other executive branch entities, particularly OMB and the NSC
- Congress, including, but not limited to, the appropriators
- State, local, and nongovernmental leadership
- The American press and public.

These relationships can be mutually supportive. Ideally, OHS would coordinate strategy and funding and resolve conflicts internally (i.e., within the administration) and work with Congress and others to promote agreed positions. This is the "team player" model. As a team player, OHS can work both directly and indirectly, through the President, OMB, and the departments and agencies,

---

[14]For example, one interviewee identified three prerequisites to successful budgetary engagement: (1) access to critical decision points in the executive branch budget process; (2) "weight in the room" (i.e., through close relationships with the President and other significant players); and (3) support from institutions outside the executive branch, particularly Congress, the press, and the public. Later in this report, we apply the interviewee's delineation of critical decision points.

[15]See Heniff (2001a) for more on the role of the President in budget development.

with Congress. To pursue this model successfully, OHS must build and maintain trust among participants. For example, the departments and agencies must be confident that their views will be heard in the coordinating process and adequately reflected, to the extent possible, in strategy and funding decisions. Moreover, Congress must believe that OHS, speaking on behalf of the administration, is making good on its word. Because the budget process repeats itself annually, a single serious episode of circumvention or weak representation could have lasting effects. The participants may be required to come back to the table later, regardless of the breach, but they may be less likely to take the process seriously or play by its rules.

Alternatively and less desirably, OHS can work with Congress to move positions that it could not move internally or those that lost the administration's support after they were introduced to Congress. This is the "independent agent" or "sniper" model. Given the need for trust in the team player model, it may be difficult to shift between the two models over time. An EOP office can be a team player or a sniper, but it cannot easily pick and choose, moment by moment. Here, we adopt the team player model, as it follows directly from the mandate of the executive order and is preferable in a policy environment where the participants, both institutions and individuals, must work together repeatedly, over an extended period.

In this report, we focus on relationships within the federal government, i.e., the executive branch and Congress; to a lesser extent, we also consider relationships with nonfederal entities, including state, local, and nongovernmental leadership. As we discuss in more detail in later sections, the nature of all these relationships will tend to change over the course of the budget cycle.

Working Within the Executive Branch

In this section, we examine leverage points within the executive branch, specifically relationships with OMB and NSC, and their importance in managing executive branch policy and budget processes. As evident post–September 11, 2001, and in the development of the President's FY 2003 budget plan, OMB can play a central role in helping OHS fulfill its coordinating role. This help can extend throughout the fiscal year, but certain "natural" limitations may set in, especially when resources are scarce. OMB and OHS are tasked with very different, and potentially conflicting, missions. During the final stages of the executive budget process, if not sooner, these two organizations may find themselves at odds, with one trying to maintain fiscal discipline while the other presses for additional resources. Partly because of these limitations, it is essential that OHS form solid relationships elsewhere in the administration.[16]

Nevertheless, for as long as the OHS/OMB alliance holds, OMB can be an important collaborator in the coordination of homeland security strategy and funding. What, more specifically, does OMB have to offer? It oversees the executive budget process, it is a repository of budgetary expertise, and it has well-established links to budget analysts in other key departments and agencies. (Although OHS will need to maintain some in-house budget expertise and develop its own network of executive branch budget contacts—at senior and staff levels—it should not waste its limited resources duplicating efforts or reinventing wheels.) Moreover, in past administrations, OMB has held regular meetings with the heads of the departments and agencies. Without appearing to co-opt the venue, OHS can use these interagency meetings to engage with officials and more effectively link the homeland security policy and budget processes.

A strong relationship between OHS and OMB would extend organizationally from top to bottom. Contacts at each level, from Director to staff, serve different purposes:

- A visibly strong relationship between OHS and OMB directors can promote cooperation at all levels across the offices and serve other important functions (e.g., by resolving significant conflicts).

- Other high- and midlevel contacts are needed to implement cooperation (e.g., by prioritizing and assigning tasks).

- Budget examiners and other professional staff provide expertise to map strategies to funding and review departments' and agencies' proposals. They also provide institutional memory. Ultimately, a purely top-down approach, absent strong staff-level ties, may lack staying power. Directors come and go, but professional staff remain to carry on the office's mission.

Similarly, OHS can form top-to-bottom relationships with other key departments and agencies. HSPD-1 will help establish these multitiered relationships, as it sets forth the organization and operation of the HSC, with forums for interagency coordination—the HSC/PC, HSC/DC, HSC/PCCs, and IWGs—at each level of contact in the departments and agencies. As we discuss in more detail below,

---

[16]To some extent, many if not most EOP relationships suffer from inherent limitations owing to differences in missions and competition for finite resources.

these relationships can improve OHS's access to the departments' and agencies' internal decisionmaking processes at critical points in the budget process.

The NSC is another obvious place to seek an alliance, given the inherent interrelatedness of NSC/OHS's policy portfolios and the President's call for their coordination on specific issues. For example, Executive Order 13228 includes requirements for coordination on detection and prevention and HSPD-1 requires that OHS and NSC colead HSC/PC meetings when "global terrorism with domestic implications is on the agenda." More generally, the NSC can be a valuable partner throughout the federal budget process, both because of its longstanding history as a policy coordinator, with established processes for bringing departments and agencies together when needed, and because of its reputation as an "honest broker." However, this relationship may also pose challenges.[17] OHS and the NSC will need to find ways to exploit, or at least accommodate, their overlapping jurisdictions—what can be a source of policymaking amity can too easily become a source of enmity.

Working with Congress

In this section, we consider leverage points within Congress and identify a "core" group of committees for outreach. Which committees constitute the core? Clearly, in a discussion of federal funding, the appropriations committees belong at the top of the list. However, OHS can also reach out strategically—throughout the year—to the authorizing and oversight committees that have been most active in this policy arena. Our analysis of committee hearings and referrals of legislative proposals identifies potential candidates for outreach.

Long before the congressional budget process begins, OHS can begin building bridges with key committees, members, and their staffs, both directly and indirectly through others in the administration. Importantly, OHS can forge these relationships regardless of whether it chooses to provide Congress with testimony. As the experience of the NSC and NEC demonstrates, it is possible to "make friends" and engender congressional support for the President's policy agenda through less-formal channels. For example, among the direct routes, the OHS Director or his staff, as appropriate, can meet regularly with interested parties to elicit their views, explain the President's policy priorities and objectives, and provide updates on the administration's strategy, programs, and activities.

---

[17]Others have noted the difficulties of forming "friendships" with the NSC, particularly when jurisdictional lines are blurry. See Orszag, Orszag, and Tyson (2001).

Each type of committee plays a different part in the policy and the budget processes, implying a different reason for OHS to make contact—some are not as obvious as others. For example, authorizing committees typically have less control over discretionary spending than do appropriating committees, but OHS can work with them to increase Congress's awareness of the President's priorities and objectives and raise public consciousness.[18] Moreover, some presidential initiatives may require new legislation prior to the enactment of funding. In these cases, the importance of close contact with the authorizing committees is more obvious.

OHS can also build bridges indirectly, through OMB and other departments and agencies. In the team player model, OHS can work with its executive branch colleagues—especially, but not only, in OMB—to gain congressional support for the President's policy agenda. For example, OMB carries out the executive branch's formal legislative coordination and clearance process. Although it is not always effective, the process covers legislative proposals, agency reports and testimony on pending legislation, statements of administration policy, and enrolled bills. Despite its shortcomings, the process offers another mechanism through which OHS—working with OMB—can coordinate the administration's homeland security message, including requests for funding. Outside this official process, OHS can also help craft departments' and agencies' testimony and other congressional communications to promote consistency with agreed administration positions. This option requires good communication between the congressional liaison in OHS and other homeland security departments and agencies.

Given the breadth of homeland security policy, we recommend that OHS proceed strategically in forming congressional alliances: first, reaching out to the committees that have been most active in this policy arena and, later, casting a wider net to expand its network. The figures in this report provide a rough gauge of committees' interest and involvement prior to and immediately following September 11. They suggest opportunities for congressional outreach, especially among the authorizing and oversight committees. However, we do not believe that this gauge is useful with respect to the appropriators; rather, we think that it is more important to consider the distribution of homeland security funding and how it relates to the subcommittees' jurisdictions. We focus on this later in the report.

---

[18]The defense authorizing committees—the Senate Armed Services and House Armed Services Committees—are noteworthy exceptions, exercising influence within their domains on par with the corresponding appropriators. Moreover, in policy arenas where mandatory spending can dominate total spending, such as in agriculture, or where fee-funded programs are especially important, the authorizing committees can play a more critical role.

To conduct this part of the analysis, we examined the frequency with which each committee held homeland security–related hearings in the 106th Congress and the first session of the 107th Congress and compared pre– and post–September 11 activity.[19] In addition, we tabulated the number and type of legislative proposals referred to each committee in the first session of the 107th Congress.[20] Although we cannot claim to have found every relevant hearing or proposal, we believe the broad trends in the data are robust. However, because the threat to homeland security is dynamic, the committees that are the most active in one session may not be the most active in the next. Thus, we offer a starting point for congressional outreach based on committees' interest, reflecting both their legislative jurisdictions and recent events.

Figures 1a–1c show the frequency of hearings in the House before and after September 11. Figure 1a allows a direct comparison of each committee's pre– and post–September 11 activity. Taken together, Figures 1b and 1c allow a comparison of the committees' pre– and post–September 11 ranks based on the number of hearings they held. They also help illustrate the extent to which congressional interest in homeland security has become more diffuse since the terrorist attacks.

---

[19]To compile our list of hearings, we conducted searches on the *Congressional Quarterly* website, http://www.oncongress.cq.com/, and on committee and subcommittee websites, using a variety of homeland security–related words and phrases. Our search period began with the opening of the 106th Congress in January 1999 and ended with the conclusion of the first session of the 107th Congress in December 2001. Within that interval, we compared pre– and post–September 11 activity, resulting in one subperiod of more than two and a half years and another of less than half a year.

Altogether we found over 200 relevant hearings, about half occurring in each subperiod. In some cases, a hearing was obviously related to homeland security and belonged on the list; however, many others required judgment calls. For the most part, we only included open hearings for which the committees or subcommittees provided enough information to determine the hearing's relevance. In a few cases, we were able to include a closed or partially closed hearing based on its title or other public information.

[20]Our list of about 180 legislative proposals is based on a *Congressional Quarterly* legislative database relating to homeland security, "Legislation on Homeland Security," available at http://www.oncongress.cq.com/, and additional searches on the *Congressional Quarterly* website and the Library of Congress website, http://thomas.loc.gov/. Our search period encompassed the entirety of the first session of the 107th Congress, roughly coinciding with 2001. We did not conduct a pre– and post–September 11 comparison.

The *Congressional Quarterly* database identifies legislation in five categories: bioterrorism and chemical weapons; emergency response and homeland strategy; intelligence gathering; protecting infrastructure; and transportation and border security. We chose to focus similarly in developing our database. For the most part, we did not include legislation on victims' compensation, financial relief as a result of the attacks, memorials, or government bonds. Although we tried to be consistent across measures of legislative activity, there are minor differences in accounting for hearings and proposals, owing partly to the data sources (for example, *Congressional Quarterly* may have been slightly more inclusive of overseas-related legislation). These differences do not appear to have had a significant effect on our findings.

13

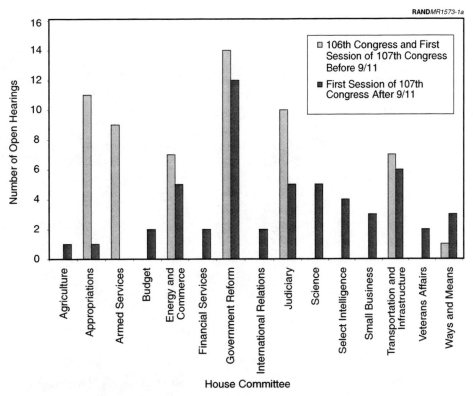

NOTE: Based on searches conducted at the *Congressional Quarterly* website and individual committee and subcommittee websites.

Figure 1a—Hearings Relating to Homeland Security Held in the U.S. House of Representatives Before and After 9/11

After September 11, the number of House committees that held hearings increased, but those committees, such as the House Government Reform Committee, that held the most hearings before the terrorist attacks and anthrax episodes also tended to hold the most hearings afterward. Two noteworthy exceptions are the House Appropriations and Armed Services Committees.[21] In past years, the Appropriations Committee has been most active during the course of the "ordinary" budget cycle; presumably it will be at least as active this year. And, as we discuss below, hearings are only one measure of congressional interest; for example, the House Appropriations Committee was deeply involved in the debate on emergency supplemental funding. The timing of the budget process and other congressional demands may also have been an important

---

[21]Another exception is the House Permanent Select Intelligence Committee, which did not hold any open hearings prior to September 11. The Select Intelligence Committee elevated the Terrorism Working Group to Subcommittee Status after the attacks. The Terrorism Subcommittee, in fact, held the four post–September 11 Select Intelligence Committee hearings.

14

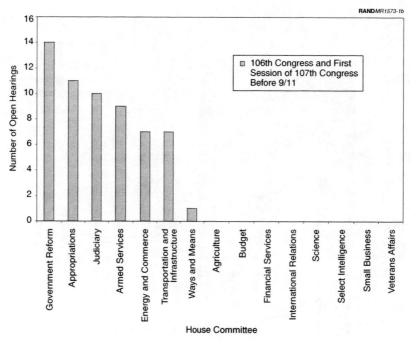

NOTE: Based on searches conducted at the *Congressional Quarterly* website and individual committee and subcommittee websites.

Figure 1b—Hearings Relating to Homeland Security Held in the U.S. House of Representatives Before 9/11

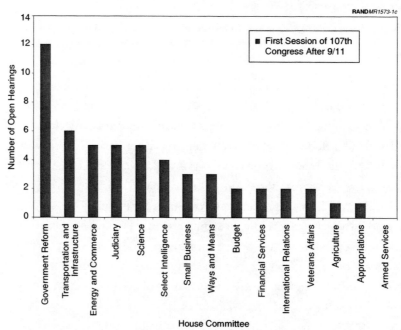

NOTE: Based on searches conducted at the *Congressional Quarterly* website and individual committee and subcommittee websites.

Figure 1c—Hearings Relating to Homeland Security Held in the U.S. House of Representatives After 9/11

factor for the House Armed Services Committee, which was addressing defense authorization and other war-related concerns following the attacks.

Figures 2a–2c allow the same kind of comparison for the Senate.

Homeland security issues also attracted broader interest in the Senate following the attacks. Among the more dramatic examples, the Senate Governmental Affairs Committee, which led the field after September 11, was not especially active before the attacks.[22] However, the Senate Appropriations Committee, unlike its House counterpart, was a significant player in both periods. Prior to September 11, nearly all of the Senate Appropriations Committee's hearings were held within the course of the ordinary budget process, as in the House; but after

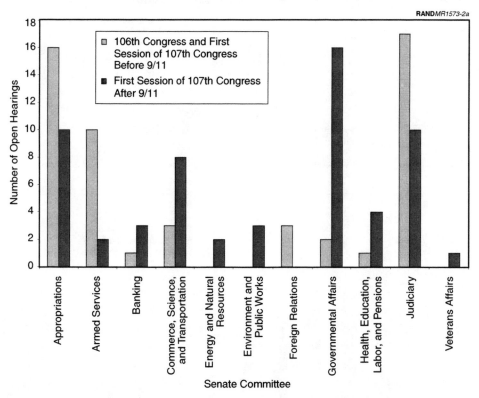

NOTE: Based on searches conducted at the *Congressional Quarterly* website and individual committee and subcommittee websites.

Figure 2a—Hearings Relating to Homeland Security Held in the U.S. Senate Before and After 9/11

---

[22]The Senate Governmental Affairs Committee held a two-part series of hearings on money-laundering in November 1999 and another three-part series in March 2001. We did not include these series in the pre–September 11 tally, as they did not substantively address homeland security or terrorism.

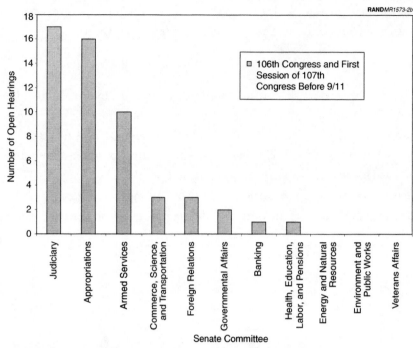

NOTE: Based on searches conducted at the *Congressional Quarterly* website and individual committee and subcommittee websites.

Figure 2b—Hearings Relating to Homeland Security Held in the U.S. Senate Before 9/11

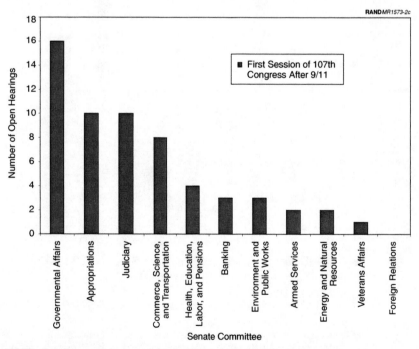

NOTE: Based on searches conducted at the *Congressional Quarterly* website and individual committee and subcommittee websites.

Figure 2c—Hearings Relating to Homeland Security Held in the U.S. Senate After 9/11

the attacks, it held several additional hearings—about half of which addressed concerns on bioterrorism. And, like its House counterpart, the Senate Armed Services Committee held relatively few homeland security hearings after September 11, also appearing to have focused on the defense authorization and other war-related activities.

Data on congressional hearings also help illustrate the ways in which a single issue can cut across committee jurisdictions. For example, we found mention of about 40 hearings focusing on issues related to bioterrorism from the start of the 106th Congress. Roughly one-half were held in each chamber. In both the House and Senate, the hearings were spread over eight committees; two committees were especially active in each. In the House, the Government Reform Committee and the Energy and Commerce Committee held the most hearings; in the Senate, the Governmental Affairs Committee and the Appropriations Committee were leaders. Although most of the bioterrorism-related hearings were held after September 11 and the anthrax episodes, several were also held before.

For a somewhat different perspective on congressional interest, we also looked at records of legislative referrals.[23] Figures 3–5 show the number of legislative proposals referred to each committee in the first session of the 107th Congress. A particular proposal may have been referred to several committees—this is especially true in the House—so that the sum of the bars in each figure does not correspond to the total number of proposals in that period. Figures 3 and 4 account for proposals relating to homeland security generally and Figure 5 looks at proposals relating to bioterrorism and chemical weapons more specifically.

However, before proceeding to the figures and analysis, a caveat on interpretation is in order. We did not attempt to rank the legislative proposals by their "importance," the extent of their consideration, or whether they passed into law. As a result, some committees may appear to have been less active than others, when, in fact, they could have been more deeply involved in a smaller number of bills that were actually enacted. The House and Senate Appropriations Committees may be two such examples. They did not see as many separate pieces of legislation as several other congressional committees, but the appropriators were enmeshed in deliberations on major bills for supplemental funding and other fiscal matters that eventually became laws.

In Figure 3, we see that the House Transportation and Infrastructure and the Judiciary Committees are clear front-runners, followed by the House Energy and

---

[23]In a small number of cases, we also matched bills with originating or reporting committees.

18

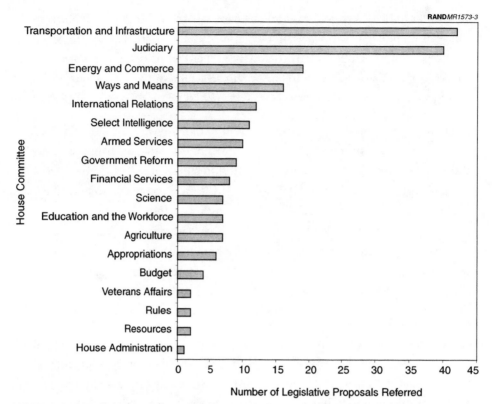

NOTE: Based on *Congressional Quarterly* (2002) legislative database and additional Web searches.

Figure 3—Legislative Proposals Relating to Homeland Security Referred to Committees of the U.S. House of Representatives in the First Session of the 107th Congress

Commerce and Ways and Means Committees. And, comparing committee activity across all three measures—pre–September 11 hearings, post–September 11 hearings, and legislative referrals—we can make some general observations about committee interest and involvement. Outside the ordinary budget process, three House committees have been especially active by all three measures: Transportation and Infrastructure, the Judiciary, and Energy and Commerce.

Figure 4 shows that three Senate committees—Commerce, Science, and Transportation; the Judiciary; and Health, Education, Labor, and Pensions— have received significantly more homeland security legislation than other Senate committees. The Senate Committee on Health, Education, Labor, and Pensions joined the ranks of the most active, owing largely to proposals on bioterrorism. This is apparent in Figure 5. Again, drawing together the results of all three measures of activity, two Senate committees have been among the most active: the Judiciary and the Commerce, Science, and Transportation Committees. After accounting for differences in committee jurisdictions, the results are similar across chambers.

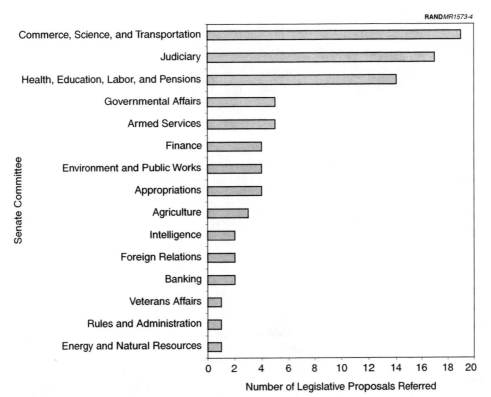

NOTE: Based on *Congressional Quarterly* (2002) legislative database and additional Web searches.

Figure 4—Legislative Proposals Relating to Homeland Security Referred to Committees of the U.S. Senate in the First Session of the 107th Congress

Judging on the basis of the referrals tabulated in Figure 5, some of the most active committees in the bioterrorism and chemical weapons arena are, perhaps not surprisingly, among the most prominent by other reckonings. The House Energy and Commerce Committee and the Senate Health, Education, Labor, and Pensions Committee clearly rank at the top of their respective chambers.[24] However, the House and Senate Agriculture Committees rank second in each chamber, admittedly, a rather distant second in the Senate. Neither of the two agricultural committees were major players by any of the other metrics used. As observed previously, we see again that a single issue like bioterrorism can cross multiple jurisdictions; however, some committees are more frequently included in the debate than others.

_____

[24]The Senate Committee on Health, Education, Labor, and Pensions was active on the basis of legislative proposals, but not especially active on the basis of its hearings.

20

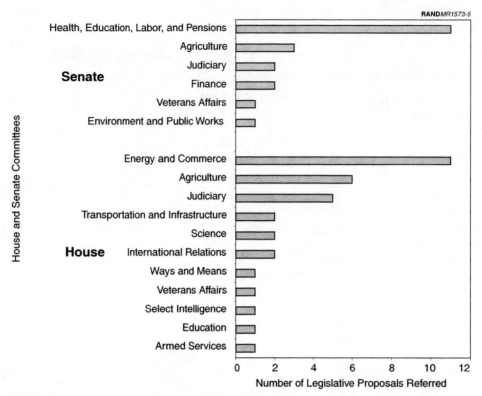

NOTE: Based on *Congressional Quarterly* (2002) legislative database and additional Web searches.

Figure 5—Legislative Proposals Relating to Bioterrorism and Chemical Weapons Referred to Committees of the U.S House of Representatives and Senate in the First Session of the 107th Congress

Taken as a whole, our analysis of congressional activity suggests a potential starting point for outreach, by identifying a group of committees that have clearly demonstrated their interest and involvement in this policy arena. Some of those committees have been active more generally, by pre– and post–September 11 metrics; others have entered the field since the attacks or have focused more narrowly on specific issues within their jurisdictions. Without neglecting this core congressional base, OHS can eventually cast a wider net to build additional support for the President's agenda outside the administration.

Which committees make up the core? Apart from the appropriators, which we address in more detail later in the report, our analysis of hearings and legislative referrals points to two Senate committees—the Judiciary and Commerce, Science, and Transportation—and three House committees—Transportation and Infrastructure, the Judiciary, and Energy and Commerce. Looking only at hearings and not referrals, we find that the House Government Reform Committee is also a clear leader; more recently, the Senate Governmental Affairs Committee has stepped to the fore. Some other committees have joined debates on specific issues, but would not make the top ranks otherwise. For example, the Senate Health, Education, Labor, and Pensions Committee and the House Agriculture Committee have seen more bioterrorism-related proposals than most other committees. The House and Senate Armed Services Committees, although less visible than others since September 11 on the basis of either hearings or proposals, warrant attention both because their earlier activity indicates long-term interest and because they are among the few authorizing committees that exercise influence within their domains on par with the corresponding appropriations subcommittees.[25]

---

[25]One example of this earlier activity in the Senate Armed Services Committee is the formation of the Subcommittee on Emerging Threats and Capabilities.

3. Relationships, Process, and Substance Intertwine

In this section we develop a model for OHS engagement that builds on the relationships that it forms with other key policy players, particularly in the administration and Congress. The model, as previously noted, is not issue specific. Instead, it is a template that can be applied to almost any of the cross-cutting issues that require OHS coordination through the HSC structure. With some modification, OHS can apply the template to either a single- or multiyear planning horizon.

Ultimately, the budgetary effect of OHS will depend on how it uses its position in the EOP and what it brings to the interagency table. To make a valuable contribution, OHS must understand the intricacies of the federal budget process, in part, to gain access to its critical decision points, and fill a role that the departments and agencies cannot fill independently. Speaking on the President's behalf, OHS is uniquely poised to bring strategy and funding decisions together across departments and agencies and provide a unified White House perspective on homeland security.

Our analysis, including the consideration of NSC, NEC, and ONDCP leadership roles, suggests three key, if deceptively simple, principles that we incorporate in a timetable for a tightly integrated interagency process:

- Establish policy priorities and objectives as early as possible

- Formulate strategy and then develop funding requests

- Be prepared for rapid change.

Although homeland security must be addressed comprehensively, OHS cannot coordinate every related policy issue, nor should it try—some issues require close interagency coordination, others require monitoring.[26] Issues along policy

---

[26]HSPD-1 identifies 11 functional areas, covering a wide range of homeland security issues. The President's FY 2003 budget focuses on four key areas, but promises a comprehensive strategy in the future. If OHS fails to distinguish between these two kinds of issues—those requiring coordination and those requiring monitoring—as it moves forward, it may eventually spread itself too thin, needlessly. This would not be unprecedented in the executive branch. For example, informal interviews suggest that this has been a problem for ONDCP. Moreover, in a discussion of drug policy coordination at state and federal levels, the RAND Drug Policy Research Center (1997) concludes, "Administrators and policymakers should . . . resist the temptation to 'coordinate

seams—i.e., those at the nexus of two or more departments' or agencies' jurisdictions—will provide the greatest challenges and merit the most time and attention. The President's budget proposal for FY 2003 provides examples of such issues in its initiatives for "Securing America's Borders" and "Defending Against Biological Terrorism." The proposal for border security cuts across the Immigration and Naturalization Service (Department of Justice), the Coast Guard (Department of Transportation), the Customs Service (Department of the Treasury), and to a lesser extent, the Animal and Plant Health Inspection Service (Department of Agriculture).

Ideally, the interagency coordination process would flow from policy priorities and objectives, to strategy formulation, to funding requests—clearly mapping budget requests to specific programs and activities. Strategy and funding coordination must be integrated, both temporally and organizationally; if not, OHS will likely fall short of producing a financially supportable interagency plan.

Our emphasis is on issue-based strategy and funding coordination. This NSC/NEC–like policy approach can complement the preparation of a consolidated homeland security budget—and vice versa—but it will not yield one on its own. OHS can add up funding across issues, but to the extent that it focuses on a subset of particular issues, it may not cover all uses of funds across all departments or agencies. Moreover, if each issue involves a different set of participants within a department or agency, the funding pieces may not come together naturally. Without an additional layer of coordination, there is some risk that OHS and the departments and agencies will lose sight of their overall commitments to homeland security.

However, we do not recommend that OHS take on the mantle of preparing a consolidated homeland security budget. For this purpose, we suggest turning to OMB, as OHS did in producing the budget estimates for *Securing the Homeland, Strengthening the Nation* (Bush, 2002a). OMB already collects and disseminates budget information on counterterrorism activities for the mandated *Annual Report to Congress on Combating Terrorism* and can request more detailed information from departments and agencies to delineate between homeland security and other counterterrorism funding. The data can be used to compile an annual consolidated budget or funding directory that would serve political and functional roles. Moreover, OHS can compare its issue-based tally with the

---

everything.'" The research further recommends that they identify "coordination clusters" which it defines as "small groups of two to five organizations . . . for which the benefits of building linkages outweigh the costs."

overall numbers provided by departments and agencies and check for consistency. Are divergences between the sum of the parts and the whole plausible? The data exercise would act as a forcing event for consideration of homeland security funding and could provide OHS with a more formal entrée to the OMB review process, without risk of draining scarce resources away from the OHS Director's primary mission.

Finally, while advance planning is essential, so is flexibility. The nature of the threat to homeland security is dynamic. If circumstances change abruptly, OHS must be able to shift gears quickly and bring the relevant departments and agencies along with it. This will be easier with an interagency strategy and funding coordination process already in place. OHS can call on the HSC, including its various subcabinet- and staff-level organizations, to devise a rapid response, including a new strategy and the supplemental funding requests to support it, as needed.

In the next two sections, we merge the foregoing discussion of relationships with these basic principles to develop a model, or road map, for effective engagement in the federal budget process that is keyed to the executive branch and congressional phases of budget formulation.

The Executive Branch Timetable

The executive branch budget process can be described as a series of critical decision points or phases, following a rough timetable that begins in the spring and ends no later than February of the following year.[27] To engage as effectively as possible, OHS requires access to each critical point or phase, starting from the very beginning of the budget process. And, the stronger its relationships within the administration, the more likely it is to gain that access.

The first critical point or phase commences when the departments and agencies begin developing their budget requests internally, usually in the spring.[28] This goes on for several months. Access to this part of the process may be especially important if OHS seeks to develop a forward-looking strategy. The second critical point or phase occurs in the fall when the departments and agencies submit their formal requests to OMB. At this time, OMB reviews their requests and returns or passes back its decisions to them. The decisions at "passback" address both the total funding of each department or agency and its allocation

---

[27] Although subject to some slippage within cycles, the executive branch budget process ends each year by the first Monday of February when the President must submit his plan to Congress.

[28] For some departments, such as the Department of Defense, the process may begin earlier.

within the department or agency. Depending on the outcome of passback, a department or agency may appeal to the OMB Director, or possibly the President, for a different level or composition of funding. The President, or his proxy, then completes the process with a final round of decisions.

Taken together, the experience of the ONDCP, NSC, and NEC and the structure of the executive branch budget process suggest a road map for effective OHS engagement. In this section we introduce a model that weds an ONDCP-like timetable to an issue-based NSC/NEC–like approach to policy coordination.[29]

ONDCP typically enters the budget process in early-to-mid spring. It issues broad guidance through the National Drug Control Strategy within the first two months of the new calendar year and then issues more specific guidance to the relevant agencies many months in advance of the President's submission to Congress (e.g., for the FY 2001 budget, it issued budget instructions and certification procedures in May 1999). ONDCP reviews agencies' budget proposals midsummer and then reviews departments' formal submissions in the fall. The intent is to coordinate budget requests and resolve differences before the process gets too far along. Although ONDCP has the authority to decertify the budget of a "National Drug Control Program agency," and may derive some benefit from the explicit threat of decertification, it is far preferable to arrive at an agreed position before the process ever reaches that point.[30] Arguably, resorting to decertification amounts to a process failure.

In its coordinating role, we recommend that OHS set the President's policy agenda no later than early spring. At that time, OHS would call together the HSC/PC, along with the OMB and NSC directors, and launch the interagency coordination process with an explicit statement of priorities and objectives. Typically, the work of strategy formulation, planning, and budgeting is conducted at lower levels, drawing on the expertise of subcabinet officials and professional staff, but cabinet-level institutional buy-in—or at the very least awareness—is essential. If the departments and agencies are on board and working together from the start, they will be more likely to speak with a single voice and stand behind funding requests later in the process. However, when conflicts arise that cannot be resolved through the interagency process, the OHS Director must have authority to call on the President.

---

[29]Daalder and Destler (2001) advocate for an NSC/NEC–like process more generally, not just with regard to strategy and funding coordination.

[30]With some qualifications, a National Drug Control Program agency is defined as "any agency that is responsible for implementing any aspect of the National Drug Control Strategy." See ONDCP (1999) citing 21 U.S.C. Section 1701(7).

Meetings at subcabinet and staff levels, including the HSC/DC, HSC/PCCs, and IWGs, that occur throughout the spring would further clarify the departments' and agencies' roles, by focusing attention on the seams of homeland security policy and formulating strategy that identifies and remedies gaps and redundancies in programs, activities, and funding. The HSC/PCCs and IWGs would generate strategy proposals and options for HSC/DC or HSC/PC decision as needed. Direct access to departments' and agencies' internal planning and decisionmaking processes, ideally through OHS participation in their deliberations, would be especially helpful beginning with the spring phase of coordination. Whether OHS gains such access would depend on the strength of its relationships with the departments and agencies. With or without access, it is important that OHS understand the internal processes of each key institution as they may differ widely and affect the form and timing of engagement.

Throughout this period, OHS must also coordinate with states, localities, and private entities—e.g., through the Federal Emergency Management Agency (FEMA) and sanctioned advisory committees at the HSC/PCC level—to advance the strategy's operability.[31] Nationwide associations of governors, municipal authorities, businesses, and nonprofit organizations may provide useful points of contact in this arena. Inclusion of these diverse communities is essential because the implementation of a national strategy may depend largely on their efforts— some of which may be partly funded through federal grants or loans—and on the consistency of their plans with federal plans. Ultimately, their buy-in may also engender support for the strategy among other policymakers.

After this early round of decisionmaking, to include OMB and NSC participants, the departments and agencies would prepare preliminary budget proposals for homeland security, thereby linking their requests to the strategy through agreed programs and activities. This would occur in July and August, during which time OMB typically issues guidance to the departments and agencies on their overall budget requests through OMB Circular No. A-11.[32] With assistance from OMB budget examiners, OHS would review the preliminary homeland security proposals for consistency with departments' and agencies' agreed positions and

---

[31]HSPD-1 states that coordination with state and local governments will occur at the HSC/PCC level. Moreover, the administration has tasked FEMA with improving the federal government's coordination with state and local governments. "FEMA will work closely with state and local officials to ensure their planning, training, and equipment needs are addressed. FEMA will also be charged with improving the federal government's coordination with state and local governments and reducing duplication with federal agencies," according to OMB (2002a), p. 18. In March 2002, after completion of the research for this report, the President established a Homeland Security Advisory Council and Senior Advisory Committees for Homeland Security. The council will provide advice and make recommendations to the President through the OHS Director.

[32]OMB Circular No. A-11 maps out the formal executive budget process with detailed directions and deadlines for submissions.

present them to the HSC/PCCs and IWGs to check for gaps, conflicts, and so on. As above, OHS would bring unresolved issues to the HSC/DC or HSC/PC, if necessary, for decision.

This coordination process would feed directly into the formal OMB budget process. It should lead to closure in early fall, when the departments and agencies submit their formal requests, embodying agreed positions, to OMB. Through this coordination process there should be no surprises in the formal submissions, so that "certification" would be a nonevent. However, it is essential that OHS have a seat at the table during OMB review and passback, any presidential appeal, and the final decisionmaking phases.

OHS has only won half the battle in coordinating departments' and agencies' submissions. It must continue to engage in the process through and beyond the OMB decisionmaking phase. But, even with a seat at the table, some important funding elements may slip away. Indeed, this is the point at which OHS and OMB are most likely to find themselves at opposite sides of the table, particularly in times of resource scarcity, and the additional support of the NSC may prove especially helpful. However, OHS is uniquely positioned to determine which elements of the departments' and agencies' formal requests are "must haves" to advise OMB as it reviews the internal composition of their submissions, and, if need be, to work with them after OMB passes back its decisions to prioritize and support their appeals.[33]

This can be described as a top-to-bottom-to-top coordination process and would make use of the HSC structure identified in HSPD-1. Guidance from the top—i.e., the President's priorities and objectives—would drive proposals and options from the bottom, which, in turn, would percolate up to the HSC/DC or HSC/PC for decision. If the HSC/PC fails to resolve an issue satisfactorily—i.e., in a way that serves the President's policy agenda—the Homeland Security Director would raise the issue with the President or his Chief of Staff, depending in part on the issue's importance. As in all such policy processes, the President is the ultimate adjudicator, but one who should be turned to sparingly.

This same process would apply whether OHS were navigating the departments and agencies through a one-year or multiyear planning process. However, the latter will be much more challenging to coordinate. Many departments and agencies do not produce "substantive" multiyear budget plans.[34] For this reason,

---

[33]Moreover, even if now at opposite sides of the table, close cooperation between OHS and OMB up to this point can lend weight to final appeals and petitions for additional resources.

[34]The Department of Defense is one noteworthy exception.

multiyear coordination would be more appropriately and productively conducted issue-by-issue than in aggregate. To elicit a department's or agency's commitment to homeland security writ large, even notionally, for several years would require considerably more information on its other commitments than may be available—at least some homeland security funding will be dual-purpose and at least some homeland security estimates will derive from shares of other estimates.[35] It may be more feasible to map out a reasonable multiyear approach for core issues; however, the effort will require more in-house OHS expertise than a one-year strategy. The departments and agencies will look to OHS to provide vision and context.

Table 1 maps this approach to critical decision points in the budget process and provides a rough timetable for implementation.

Participation in the Congressional Budget Process

Here we focus on the period after the President submits his budget and Congress begins consideration of its own version. Like the executive branch process, the congressional process follows a rough timetable. Loosely speaking, it begins with the President's submission, no later than the first Monday of February, and usually concludes with a series of appropriations bills, preferably signed into law before the start of the next fiscal year. However, the congressional process is subject to even more slippage than the executive branch process. For a particularly dramatic example, Congress enacted 14 continuing resolutions for FY 1996, compared with an average of three per year for FY 1997 through FY 1999 (Streeter, 1999, p. 16).

After the President's submission, the Budget Committees begin work on the Budget Resolution. These committees establish congressional priorities by setting ceilings for each of the 20 major functional categories.[36] At this stage in the process, OHS has an opportunity to present a unified policy perspective. This may be its first and last chance to present this kind of perspective to Congress. Later, consideration of funding is parsed according to the jurisdictions of the 13 appropriations subcommittees in each chamber. Because these subcommittees are not organized along programmatic lines, funding requests for a well-coordinated homeland security strategy will eventually face a series of

---

[35]See Murphy (1994) and Murphy et al. (2000).

[36]Until recently, the Budget Committees' decisions were more limited by discretionary spending caps. Limits on highway, mass transit, and other discretionary spending were set through FY 2002; limits on conservation spending extend through FY 2006.

Table 1

Proposed OHS Activity in the Executive Budget Process

Calendar Year Prior to the Year in Which Fiscal Year Begins			
Time Period	*Current Executive Branch Activity*		Proposed OHS Activity
	General[a]	ONDCP[b]	
Feb.– March	N/A	ONDCP issues National Drug Control Strategy, including strategic goals and objectives.	OHS specifies objectives and priorities, focusing on core issues that require interagency coordination; convenes cabinet-level interagency meeting through HSC/PC, with OMB and NSC directors attending, to set policy agenda.
April– June	Agencies begin development of budget requests. The President, with the assistance of OMB, reviews and makes policy decisions for the budget that begins October 1 of the following year.	ONDCP issues process guidance to departmental budget directors, augmenting the general policy guidance provided in the National Strategy; meets with senior budget officials from departments and agencies; develops and proposes agency drug initiatives; issues additional guidance to cabinet officers on funding priorities for specific initiatives; begins summer budget certification and review process for certain agencies, bureaus, and programs.	OHS leads issue-based HSC/PCCs and IWGs, with OMB and NSC participation, to formulate and coordinate interagency strategy and identify funding requirements for programs and activities; coordinates with FEMA and consults advisory committees and associations for state, local, and private sector input at HSC/PCC level; presents proposal or options to HSC/DC or HSC/PC.
July– Aug.	OMB issues policy directions to agencies, providing guidance for agencies' formal budget requests.	ONDCP continues summer budget process; prepares pre-certification letters for departments; meets with cabinet officers to discuss funding priorities prior to OMB submission.	Agencies prepare preliminary budget proposals, linking funding to strategy through agreed programs and activities; OHS policy and budget staff review preliminary proposals with OMB staff assistance; OHS presents unified perspective to HSC/PCCs and IWGs, using meetings to

Table 1—continued

Time Period	General[a]	ONDCP[b]	Proposed OHS Activity
July–Aug. (cont.)			address conflicts, gaps, etc., and raises any unresolved issues to the HSC/DC or HSC/PC if needed; checks for consistency with OMB aggregate funding report.
Early fall	Agencies submit initial budget requests to OMB.	ONDCP begins fall budget certification review process; receiving departments' proposals prior to OMB.	OHS staff reviews agencies' formal budget submissions, working closely with OMB staff, and certifies adequacy to OMB Director.
Nov.–Dec.	OMB and the President review and make decisions on agencies' requests, referred to as OMB "passback"; following passback, agencies identify shortfalls and prioritize appeals; agencies may appeal these decision to the OMB Director, and in some cases directly to the President.	ONDCP issues certification letters and makes final budget recommendations.	OHS participates in senior-level reviews with OMB and NSC; OHS works with agencies after passback, one-on-one or together, to identify remaining shortfalls and prioritize appeals; OHS petitions the President directly if necessary.

Calendar Year in Which Fiscal Year Begins			
Time Period	Current Executive Branch Activity		Proposed OHS Activity
	General[a]	ONDCP[b]	
February	President submits budget—no later than the first Monday of February—to Congress; OMB coordinates roll out.	ONDCP issues National Drug Control Strategy, including proposed national drug control budget.	OHS provides executive support and engages in public outreach through speeches, press statements, fact sheets, etc., presenting unified policy perspective.

Table 1—continued

Time Period	General[a]	ONDCP[b]	Proposed OHS Activity
Feb.– Sept.	Congressional phase: Agencies interact with Congress, justifying and explaining President's budget.	Congressional phase: Agencies interact with Congress, justifying and explaining President's budget.	OHS briefs Congress, including but not limited to the leadership and appropriating committees, and interacts indirectly, through the President, OMB, and departments and agencies.
October 1	Fiscal year begins.	Fiscal year begins.	Fiscal year begins.
Oct.– Sept.	OMB apportions funds to agencies. Agencies incur obligations and make outlays.	—	OHS monitors strategy; develops supplemental requests with OMB and through the interagency coordination process, as necessary.

[a] From Heniff (1999).
[b] From U.S. General Accounting Office (1999).
NOTE: FEMA = Federal Emergency Management Agency; HSC = Homeland Security Council; HSC/PC = HSC/Principals Committee; HSC/DC = HSC/Deputies Committee; HSC/PCC = HSC/Policy Coordination Committee; IWG = interagency working group; OHS = Office of Homeland Security; OMB = Office of Management and Budget; ONDCP = Office of National Drug Control Policy.

fragmented appropriations decisions. Decisions about funding for one issue can and often do span several subcommittees. For example, the President's initiative for border security in the FY 2003 budget proposal not only spans four departments, but also extends to several appropriations subcommittees. As discussed previously, OHS can approach these committees directly and indirectly, especially through OMB, which already has a clear role in this process.

Following the Budget Resolution, or sooner, the focus of the legislative process shifts to the Senate and House appropriators.[37] Although nearly all 13 subcommittees have at least some financial control over homeland security policy, some are more relevant than others—measured in terms of their shares of discretionary funding. Figure 6 shows each subcommittee's approximate share of estimated and proposed discretionary homeland security funding for FY 2001, FY 2002, and proposed FY 2003, as reported in February 2002, with supplemental funding.[38] The figure suggests potential subcommittee focal points for OHS attention.

---

[37] For more on the timing of the congressional process, see Heniff (1998) and Streeter (1999).

[38] Our data source for this figure is OMB (2002c). We apportion the departments' and agencies' FY 2001, FY 2002, and proposed FY 2003 homeland security funding to their corresponding appropriation s subcommittees by approximation. Absent more detail, we attribute "national

32

Figure 6 is only a partial indicator of the appropriators' importance. It shows six subcommittees accounting for the largest shares of the homeland security "pie"—one that will nearly double in size between FY 2001 and FY 2003, if the President's FY 2003 proposal is accepted. Four subcommittees—Defense; Commerce, Justice, State, and the Judiciary; Transportation; and Treasury, Postal, and General Government—were prominent in all three years. Two other subcommittees—Labor, Health and Human Services, and Education; and Veterans Affairs, Housing and Urban Development, and Independent Agencies—emerged later.[39] However, funding shares and policy priorities are

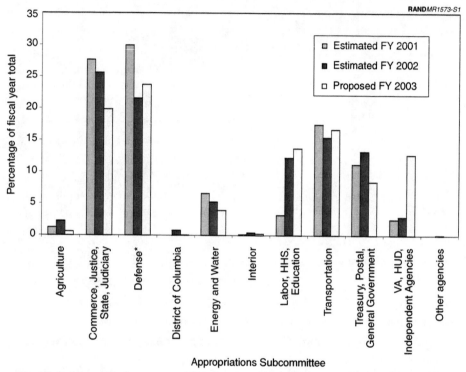

NOTE: Derived from OMB Department and Agency Estimates and Requests as of February 2002, with FY 2001 and FY 2002 Supplemental Funding.
*Funding attributed to the Defense Subcommittee may include some funding ordinarily associated with the Military Construction Subcommittee.

Figure 6—Approximate Shares of Discretionary Homeland Security Funding by Appropriations Subcommittee

security" funding to the Defense Subcommittee (although it may also include some funding ordinarily associated with other subcommittees, including the Military Construction Subcommittee). We also attribute a modest amount of funding for State/International activities to the Commerce, Justice, State, and the Judiciary Subcommittee. Some of that funding may, in fact, belong under Foreign Operations. For comparison, we repeated this exercise without the FY 2001 and FY 2002 supplemental funding and it did not change the story greatly. In March 2002, the President submitted a new supplemental appropriations request for FY 2002, amounting to $5.2 billion. It is not reflected in Figure 6. The main effect of including it would be to increase the Transportation Subcommittee's FY 2002 funding share.

[39]The record of hearings in the House and Senate shows a similar pattern, albeit with less activity than might be expected under the Transportation Subcommittees.

not perfectly correlated. Measures that do not map to any of the top six subcommittees may also require attention; some may also involve mandatory spending or require a change of law to implement them, thereby raising the level of importance of engagement with the authorizing committees. Finally, and as noted previously, the threat to homeland security is dynamic. New issues may emerge over time and others may be put to rest.[40] Thus, a subcommittee that appears to be less interested today may be more interested in the future and vice versa.

On the basis of Figure 6 or a similar assessment of future funding needs, OHS can focus its outreach efforts on appropriations subcommittees that are relevant to the current or anticipated homeland security strategy. It can approach these subcommittees through the direct and indirect channels previously identified, possibly drawing on its relationships with other core committees to help shed light on policy priorities and objectives and raise public awareness. Independent of OHS, nonfederal entities that have a stake in the strategy might seek to promote such awareness to obtain federal funding for their related programs and activities.

---

[40]Some issues may be "put to rest" through large up-front expenditures, possibly resulting in anomalously large shares for some subcommittees in particular years.

4. Conclusions

In this report, we have identified several of the key players in the homeland security arena in both the administration and Congress and have set out a road map for effective engagement in the federal budget process. We find that the ability of OHS to secure department and agency funding for agreed programs and activities in support of the President's policy agenda would depend, in large part, on the strength of its relationships with the President and with other key institutions and their proponents. Process is largely about people and alliances.

In Congress, a modest number of committees appear to dominate the homeland security playing field, both within the realm of appropriations and outside it, but many others have demonstrated an interest. Some active committees are "new entrants" to this policy arena, owing to its elevated status, and others have been less visible because they tend to focus on a specific subset of related issues. Thus, OHS can build on a core congressional base and eventually cast its net more widely. Without neglecting that core, OHS can cultivate new congressional interest to build support for the President's policy agenda and to strengthen its position in the EOP.

In determining how to use its relationships within the administration and with Congress, we recommend focusing on those issues that genuinely require coordination, thereby filling a policymaking vacuum, and participating in each critical decision point or phase in the budget process to draw together strategy and funding across multiple jurisdictions. In all likelihood, OHS will have an easier time as a coordinator to the extent that it still benefits from political goodwill, in both the executive branch and Congress, and while funding is readily available—departments and agencies tend to be more cooperative when real resources are on the table. If OHS can put a policy process in place when goodwill and resources are on its side, it may be able to carry over that process into leaner times.

Bibliography

Belasco, Amy, and Larry Nowels, "Terrorism Funding: Congressional Debate on Emergency Supplemental Allocations," Congressional Research Service, RL31187, January 7, 2002.

Belluck, Pam, and Timothy Egan, "A Nation Challenged—Domestic Defense: Cities and States Say Confusion and Cost Hamper Security Drive," *New York Times*, December 10, 2001, p. B1.

Bettelheim, Adriel, "Security Funding Effort Will Require Deft Touch by Ridge," *CQ Daily Monitor*, Vol. 38, No. 15A, February 7, 2002, p. 7.

Bush, President George W., "Establishing the Office of Homeland Security and the Homeland Security Council," Executive Order 13228, October 8, 2001.

_____, Homeland Security Presidential Directive–1: "Organization and Operation of the Homeland Security Council," October 29, 2001a.

_____, Homeland Security Presidential Directive–2: "Combating Terrorism Through Immigration Policies," October 29, 2001b.

_____, *Securing the Homeland, Strengthening the Nation*, 2002a.

_____, "Establishing the President's Homeland Security Advisory Council and Senior Advisory Committees for Homeland Security," Executive Order 13260, March 21, 2002b.

Carnevale, John, and Patrick Murphy, "Matching Rhetoric to Dollars: Twenty-Five Years of Federal Drug Strategies and Budgets," *Journal of Drug Issues*, Vol. 29, No. 2, Spring 1999, p. 299.

Congressional Quarterly, "Legislation on Homeland Security," available online at http://www.oncongress.cq.com (accessed February 6, 2002).

Daalder, Ivo H., and I. M. Destler, "Organizing for Homeland Security," Statement Before the Committee on Government Affairs, U.S. Senate, October 12, 2001.

Heniff, Bill, Jr., "The Congressional Budget Process Timetable," Congressional Research Service, 98-472, May 18, 1998.

_____, "The Executive Budget Process Timetable," Congressional Research Service, RS20152, April 8, 1999.

_____, "Formulation and Content of the Budget Resolution," Congressional Research Service, 98-512-GOV, February 7, 2000.

_____, "The Role of the President in Budget Development," Congressional Research Service, RS20179, March 5, 2001a.

36

_____, "Discretionary Spending Limits," Congressional Research Service, RS20008, March 19, 2001b.

Kosiak, Steven M., "U.S. Funding for Homeland Defense and Combating Terrorism," Center for Strategic and Budgetary Assessment, January 24, 2002.

Murphy, P. J., "Keeping Score: The Frailties of the Federal Drug Budget," Santa Monica, Calif.: RAND, IP-138, 1994.

Murphy, P. J., Lynn E. Davis, Timothy Liston, David E. Thaler, and Kathi Webb, *Improving Anti-Drug Budgeting*, Santa Monica, Calif.: RAND, MR-1262-ONDCP/NSF, 2000.

Office of Management and Budget, *Budget of the United States Government, Fiscal Year 2003*, February 2002a.

_____, "President Submits $27.1 Billion Emergency FY 2002 Supplemental Appropriations Request," Press Release, March 21, 2002b.

_____, *FY 2003 Budget Briefing Book*, Summary Tables, 2002c.

Office of National Drug Control Policy, "ONDCP Circular: Budget Instructions and Certification Procedures," May 5, 1999.

OMB—*See* Office of Management and Budget.

ONDCP—*See* Office of National Drug Control Policy.

Orszag, Jonathan M., Peter R. Orszag, and Laura D. Tyson, "The Process of Economic Policy-Making During the Clinton Administration," July 2001, paper to be included in Jeffrey Frankel and Peter R. Orszag, eds., *American Policy in the 1990s*, Cambridge, Mass.: MIT Press, forthcoming.

Pianin, Eric, and Bill Miller, "For Ridge, Ambition and Realities Clash," *Washington Post*, January 23, 2002, p. A1.

PriceWaterhouseCoopers, "Management Review of the Office of National Drug Control Policy: Final Report to the U.S. General Accounting Office," June 2000.

RAND Drug Policy Research Center, "Coordinating Drug Policy at the State and Local Levels," Santa Monica, Calif.: RAND, RB-6005, 1997.

Relyea, Harold C. "Homeland Security: The Presidential Coordination Office," Congressional Research Service, RL31148, October 10, 2001.

Streeter, Sandy, "The Congressional Appropriations Process: An Introduction," Congressional Research Service, 97-684-GOV, August 3, 1999.

U.S. Congressional Budget Office, "Homeland Security," in Chapter Seven, *The Budget and Economic Outlook: Fiscal Years 2003–2012*, January 2002.

U.S. Department of State, Office of the Historian, "History of the National Security Council, 1947–1997," August 1997.

U.S. General Accounting Office, *ONDCP Efforts to Manage the National Drug Control Budget*, GAO/GGD-99-80, May 1999.

_____, "Homeland Security, Challenges and Strategies in Addressing Short- and Long-Term National Needs," GAO-02-160T, Statement of David M. Walker, November 7, 2001, p. 6.

U.S. Government Printing Office, "Title VII Office of National Drug Control Policy Reauthorization Act of 1998."